A Soldier of th

Edward Morlae

Alpha Editions

This edition published in 2023

ISBN : 9789357966634

Design and Setting By
Alpha Editions
www.alphaedis.com
Email - info@alphaedis.com

PREFACE

When Sergeant Morlae turned up at the *Atlantic* office and, with his head cocked on one side, remarked ingratiatingly, "I'm told this is the highest-toned office in the United States," there was nothing to do but to assure him he was right and to make him quite comfortable while he told his wonderful story. That story, however, was not told consecutively, but in chapters as his crowding recollections responded to the questions of his interlocutor. It was a story, too, which could not be told at a sitting, and it was not until the evening of the second day that Sergeant Morlae recounted the exploit which won the Croix de Guerre pinned to his chest—a cross which he said, with the sole touch of personal pride noticed in three days passed largely in his company, had above it not the copper but the silver clasp.

Sergeant Morlae is a Dirk Hatteraick of a man to look at, and the education of that beloved pirate was no more rugged than his own. His father was a Frenchman born who had seen service in '70 and won a captain's commission in the "Terrible Year." After the war, Morlae, senior, settled in this country and his son was born in California. As young Morlae grew up, finding the family business of contracting on a small scale somewhat circumscribed, he sought more hazardous employment in active service in the Philippines and in more than one civilian "scrap" in Mexico. It was good training. August, 1914, found him again in Los Angeles. For two days his French blood mounted as he read the newspapers, and on the morning of August 3 he packed his grip and started for Paris to enlist in the Legion. Since he had already seen service, he was soon made a corporal and later a sergeant. Morlae, says a letter from a Harvard graduate who served under him in those days, was "an excellent soldier," "a strong, efficient, ambitious man," though, as the reader of this and letters from other Legionaries may infer, he was neither sentimental in his methods nor supersensitive with his men. Maintaining discipline in so motley a crew as the Legion is rather a rasping process, and Sergeant Morlae was born disqualified for diplomatic service. Future reunions of La Légion are likely to lack the sweet placidity which wraps the Grand Army of the Republic on the anniversaries of Chancellorsville and Gettysburg.

But to the story. The things that war is are not often told except in generalization or in words of fanciful rhetoric. It would be hard to find elsewhere, crammed into a brief narrative, so much of the sense of actuality—that realism made perfect which even readers who have known no such experience feel instinctively is true. Yet the story is not made of horror. The essence of its life is the spirit that delights in peril. The "Soldier of the Legion" has in it that spinal thrill which has electrified great tales of battle since blood was first let and ink spilled to celebrate it.

ELLERY SEDGWICK.

I

One day during the latter part of August, 1915, my regiment, the 2me Étranger (Foreign Legion), passed in review before the President of the French Republic and the commander-in-chief of her armies, General Joffre. On that day, after twelve months of fighting, the regiment was presented by President Poincaré with a battle-flag. The occasion marked the admission of the Légion Étrangère to equal footing with the regiments of the line. Two months later—it was October 28—the remnants of this regiment were paraded through the streets of Paris, and, with all military honors, this same battle-flag was taken across the Seine to the Hôtel des Invalides. There it was decorated with the cross of the Legion of Honor, and, with reverent ceremony, was placed between the flag of the cuirassiers who died at Reichshofen and the equally famous standard which the Garibaldians bore in 1870-71. The flag lives on. The regiment has ceased to exist.

On the battlefield of La Champagne, from Souain to the Ferme Navarin, from Somme Py to the Butte de Souain, the ground is thickly studded with low wooden crosses and plain pine boards marked with the Mohammedan crescent and star. Beside the crosses you see bayonets thrust into the ground, and dangling from their cross-bars little metal disks which months ago served their purpose in identifying the dead and now mark their graves. Many mounds bear no mark at all. On others again you see a dozen helmets laid in rows, to mark the companionship of the dead below in a common grave. It is there you will find the Legion.

Of the Legion I can tell you at first-hand. It is a story of adventurers, of criminals, of fugitives from justice. Some of them are drunkards, some thieves, and some with the mark of Cain upon them find others to keep them company. They are men I know the worst of. And yet I am proud of them—proud of having been one of them; very proud of having commanded some of them.

It is all natural enough. Most men who had come to know them as I have would feel as I do. You must reckon the good with the evil. You must remember their comradeship, their *esprit de corps*, their pathetic eagerness to serve France, the sole country which has offered them asylum, the country which has shown them confidence, mothered them, and placed them on an equal footing with her own sons. These things mean something to a man who has led the life of an outcast, and the Légionnaires have proved their loyalty many times over. At Arras there are more than four hundred kilometres of trench-line which they have restored to France. The Legion has always boasted that it never shows its back, and the Legion has made good.

In my own section there were men of all races and all nationalities. There were Russians and Turks, an Annamite and a Hindu. There were Frenchmen from God knows where. There was a German, God only knows why. There were Bulgars, Serbs, Greeks, negroes, an Italian, and a Fiji Islander fresh from an Oxford education,—a silent man of whom it was whispered that he had once been an archbishop,—three Arabians, and a handful of Americans who cared little for the quiet life. As Bur-bekkar, the Arabian bugler, used to say in his bad French, "Ceux sont le ra-ta international"—"They're the international stew."

Many of the men I came to know well. The Italian, Conti, had been a professional bicycle-thief who had slipped quietly into the Legion when things got too hot for him. When he was killed in Champagne he was serving his second enlistment. Doumergue, a Frenchman who was a particularly good type of soldier, had absconded from Paris with his employer's money and had found life in the Legion necessary to his comfort. A striking figure with a black complexion was Voronoff, a Russian prince whose precise antecedents were unknown to his mates. Pala was a Parisian "Apache" and looked the part. Every man had left a past behind him. But the Americans in the Legion were of a different type. Some of us who volunteered for the war loved fighting, and some of us loved France. I was fond of both.

But even the Americans were not all of one stripe. J. J. Casey had been a newspaper artist, and Bob Scanlon, a burly negro, an artist with his fist in the squared ring. Alan Seeger had something of the poet in him. Dennis Dowd was a lawyer; Edwin Bouligny a lovable adventurer. There was D. W. King, the sprig of a well-known family. William Thaw, of Pittsburg, started with us, though he joined the Flying Corps later on. Then there were James Bach, of New York; B. S. Hall, who hailed from Kentucky; Professor Ohlinger, of Columbia; Phelizot, who had shot enough big game in Africa to feed the regiment. There were Delpeuch, and Capdeveille, and little Tinkard, from New York. Bob Soubiron came, I imagine, from the United States in general, for he had been a professional automobile racer. The Rockwell brothers, journalists, signed on from Georgia; and last, though far from least, was Friedrich Wilhelm Zinn, from Battle Creek, Michigan.

The rest of the section were old-time Légionnaires, most of them serving their second enlistment of five years, and some their third. All these were seasoned soldiers, veterans of many battles in Algiers and Morocco. My section—complete—numbered sixty. Twelve of us survive, and of these there are several still in the hospital recovering from wounds. Zinn and Tinkard lie there with bullets in their breasts; Dowd, with his right arm nearly severed; Soubiron, shot in the leg; Bouligny, with a ball in his stomach. But Bouligny, like many another, is an old hand in the hospital. He has been there twice before with metal to be cut out. Several others lie totally incapacitated from wounds, and more than half of the section rests quietly along the route of the regiment. Seven of them are buried at Craonne; two more at Ferme Alger, near Rheims. Eighteen of them I saw buried myself in Champagne.

That is the record of the first section of Company I. Section III, on the night of the first day's fighting in Champagne, mustered eight men out of the forty-two who had fallen into line that morning. Section IV lost that day more than half of its effectives. Section II lost seventeen out of thirty-eight. War did its work thoroughly with the Legion. We had the place of honor in the attack, and we paid for it.

II

Two days before the forward movement began, we were informed by our captain of the day and hour set for the attack. We were told the exact number of field-pieces and heavy guns which would support us and the number of shells to be fired by each piece. Our artillery had orders to place four shells per metre per minute along the length of the German lines. Our captain gave us also very exact information regarding the number of German batteries opposed to us. He even told us the regimental numbers of the Prussian and Saxon regiments which were opposite our line. From him we learned also that along the whole length of our first row of trenches steps had been cut into the front bank in order to enable us to mount it without delay, and that our own barbed-wire entanglements, which were immediately in front of this trench, had been pierced by lanes cut through every two metres, so that we might advance without the slightest hindrance.

On the night of September 23, the commissioned officers, including the colonel of the regiment, entered the front lines of trenches, and with stakes marked the front to be occupied by our regiment during the attack. It was like an arrangement for a race. Starting from the road leading from Souain to Vouziers, the officers, after marking the spot with a big stake, paced fifteen hundred metres to the eastward and there marked the extreme right of the regiment's position by a second stake. Midway between these two a third was placed. From the road to the stake, the seven hundred and fifty metres marked the terrain for Battalion C. The other seven hundred and fifty metres bearing to the left were assigned to Battalion D. Just one hundred metres behind these two battalions a line was designated for Battalion E, which was to move up in support.

My own company formed the front line of the extreme left flank of the regiment. Our left was to rest on the highroad and our front was to run from that to a stake marking a precise frontage of two hundred metres. From these stakes, which marked the ends of our line, we were ordered to take a course due north, sighting our direction by trees and natural objects several kilometres in the rear of the German lines. These were to serve us for guides during the advance. After all these matters had been explained to us at length, other details were taken up with the engineers, who were shown piles of bridging, ready made in sections of planking so that they might be readily placed over the German trenches and thus permit our guns and supply-wagons to cross quickly in the wake of our advance.

The detail was infinite, but everything was foreseen. Twelve men from each company were furnished with long knives and grenades. Upon these "trench-cleaners," as we called them, fell the task of entering the German trenches and caves and bomb-proofs, and disposing of such of the enemy as were still hidden therein after we had stormed the trench and passed on to the other side. All extra shoes, all clothing and blankets were turned in to the quartermaster, and each man was provided with a second canteen of water, two days of "iron rations," and one hundred and thirty rounds additional, making two hundred and fifty cartridges per man. The gas-masks and mouth-pads were ready; emergency dressings were inspected, and each man ordered to put on clean underwear and shirts to prevent possible infection of the wounds.

One hour before the time set for the advance, we passed the final inspection and deposited our last letters with the regimental postmaster. Those letters meant a good deal to all of us and they were in our minds during the long wait that followed. One man suddenly began to intone the "Marseillaise." Soon every man joined in singing. It was a very Anthem of Victory. We were ready, eager, and confident: for us to-morrow held but one chance—Victory.

III

Slowly the column swung out of camp, and slowly and silently, without a spoken word of command, it changed its direction to the right and straightened out its length upon the road leading to the trenches. It was 10 P.M. precisely by my watch. The night was quite clear, and we could see, to right and to left, moving columns marching parallel to ours. One, though there was not quite light enough to tell which, was our sister regiment, the 1er Régiment Étranger. The other, as I knew, was the 8me Zouaves. The three columns marched at the same gait. It was like a funeral march, slow and very quiet. There was no singing and shouting; none of the usual badinage. Even the officers were silent. They were all on foot, marching like the rest of us. We knew there would be no use for horses to-morrow.

AS THEY SWUNG INTO COLUMN THE NIGHT BEFORE THE
25th OF SEPTEMBER

To-morrow was the day fixed for the grand attack. There was not a man in the ranks who did not know that to-morrow, at 9.15, was the time set. Every man, I suppose, wondered whether he would do or whether he would die. I wondered myself.

I did not really think I should die. Yet I had arranged my earthly affairs. "One can never tell," as the French soldier says with a shrug. I had written to my friends at home. I had named the men in my company to whom I wished to leave my personal belongings. Sergeant Velte was to have my Parabellum pistol; Casey my prismatics; Birchler my money-belt and its contents; while Sergeant Jovert was booked for my watch and compass. Yet, in the back of my mind, I smiled at my own forethought. I *knew* that I should come out alive. I recalled to myself the numerous times that I had been in imminent peril: in the Philippines, in Mexico, and during the thirteen months of this war. I could remember time and again when men were killed on each side of me and I escaped unscratched. Take the affair of Papoin, Joly, and Bob Scanlon. We were standing together so near that we could have clasped hands. Papoin was killed, Joly was severely wounded, and Scanlon was hit in the ankle—all by the same shell. The fragments which killed and wounded the first two passed on one side of me, while the piece of iron that hit Bob went close by my other side. Yet I was untouched! Again, take the last patrol. When I was out of cover, the Germans shot at me from a range of ten metres—and missed! I felt certain that my day was not to-morrow.

Just the same, I was glad that my affairs were arranged, and it gave me a sense of conscious satisfaction to think that my comrades would have something to remember me by. There is always the chance of something unforeseen happening.

The pace was accelerating. The strain was beginning to wear off. From right and left there came a steady murmur of low talk. In our own column men were beginning to chaff each other. I could distinctly hear Soubiron describing in picturesque detail to Capdeveille how he, Capdeveille, would look, gracefully draped over the German barbed wire; and I could hear Capdeveille's heated response that he would live long enough to spit upon Soubiron's grave; and I smiled to myself. The moment of depression and self-communication had passed. The men had found themselves and were beginning their usual chaffing. And yet, in all their chatter there seemed to be an unusually sharp note. The jokes all had an edge to them. References to one another's death were common, and good wishes for one another's partial dismemberment excited only laughter. Just behind me I heard King express the hope that if he lost an arm or a leg he would at least get the *médaille militaire* in exchange. By way of comfort, his chum, Dowd, remarked that, whether he got the medal or not, he was very sure of getting a permit to beg on the street-corners.

From personal bickerings we passed on to a discussion of the Germans and German methods of making war. We talked on the finer points of hand-grenades, poison gas, flame-projectors, vitriol bombs, and explosive bullets. Everybody seemed to take particular pleasure in describing the horrible wounds caused by the different weapons. Each man embroidered upon the tales the others told.

We were marching into hell. If you judged them by their conversation, these men must have been brutes at heart, worse than any "Apache"; and yet of those around me several were university graduates; one was a lawyer; two were clerks; one a poet of standing; one an actor; and there were several men of leisure, Americans almost all of them.

The talk finally settled upon the Germans. Many and ingenious were the forms of torture invented upon the spur of the moment for the benefit of the "Boches." "Hanging is too good for them," said Scanlon. After a long discussion, scalping alive seemed the most satisfactory to the crowd.

It had come to be 11 P.M. We were at the mouth of the communicating trench and entering it, one by one. Every so often, short transverse trenches opened up to right and left, each one crammed full of soldiers. Talking and laughing stopped. We continued marching along the trench, kilometre after kilometre, in utter silence. As we moved forward, the lateral trenches became more numerous. Every fifteen to eighteen feet we came to one running from right to left, and each was filled with troops, their arms grounded. As we filed slowly by, they looked at us enviously. It was amusing to see how curious they looked, and to watch their whispering as we passed. Why should we precede them in attack?

"Who are you?" several men asked.

"La Légion."

"A-a-ah, la Légion! That explains it."

Our right to the front rank seemed to be acknowledged. It did every man of us good.

We debouched from the trench into the street of a village. It was Souain. Houses, or ghosts of houses, walled us in on each side. Through the windows and the irregular shell-holes in the walls, the stars twinkled; while through a huge gap in the upper story of one of the houses I caught a glimpse of the moon, over my right shoulder. Lucky omen! "I'll come through all right," I repeated to myself, and rapped with my knuckle upon the rifle-stock, lest the luck break.

Not one house in the village was left standing—only bare walls. Near the end of the street, in the midst of chaos, we passed a windmill. The gaunt steel frame still stood. I could see the black rents in the mill and the great arms where the shrapnel had done its work; but still the wheel turned, slowly, creaking round and round, with its shrill metal scream.

The column turned to the left and again disappeared in a trench. After a short distance we turned to the right, then once more to the left, then on, and finally, not unwillingly, we came to a rest. We did not have to be told that we were now in the front line, for through the rifle-ports we could see the French shells bursting ahead of us like Fourth-of-July rockets.

The artillery had the range perfectly, and the shells, little and big, plumped with pleasing regularity into the German trenches. The din was indescribable—almost intolerable. Forty, even fifty, shells per minute were falling into a space about a single kilometre square. The explosions sounded almost continuous, and the return fire of the Germans seemed almost continuous. Only the great ten-inch long-range Teuton guns continued to respond effectively.

We looked at the show for a while, and then lay down in the trench. Every man used his knapsack for a pillow and tried to snatch a few hours' sleep. It was not a particularly good place for a nervous sleeper, but we were healthy and pretty tired.

The next morning, at 8 A.M., hot coffee was passed round, and we breakfasted on sardines, cheese, and bread, with the coffee to wash it down. At 9 the command passed down the line, "Every man ready!" Up went the knapsack on every man's back, and, rifle in hand, we filed along the trench.

The cannonading seemed to increase in intensity. From the low places in the parapet we caught glimpses of barbed wire which would glisten in occasional flashes of light. Our own we could plainly see, and a little farther beyond was the German wire.

Suddenly, at the sound of a whistle, we halted. The command, "Baïonnette au canon!" passed down the section. A drawn-out rattle followed, and the bayonets were fixed. Then the whistle sounded again. This time twice. We adjusted our straps. Each man took a look at his neighbor's equipment. I turned and shook hands with the fellows next to me. They were grinning, and I felt my own nerves a-quiver as we waited for the signal.

Waiting seemed an eternity. As we stood there a shell burst close to our left. A moment later it was whispered along the line that an adjutant and five men had gone down.

What were we waiting for? I glanced at my watch. It was 9.15 exactly. The Germans evidently had the range. Two more shells burst close to the same place. We inquired curiously who was hit this time. Our response was two whistles. That was our signal. I felt my jaws clenching, and the man next to me looked white. It was only for a second. Then every one of us rushed at the trench wall, each and every man struggling to be the first out of the trench. In a moment we had clambered up and out. We slid over the parapet, wormed our way through gaps in the wire, formed in line, and, at the command, moved forward at march-step straight toward the German wire.

The world became a roaring hell. Shell after shell burst near us, sometimes right among us; and, as we moved forward at the double-quick, men fell right and left. We could hear the subdued rattling of the mitrailleuses and the roar of volley fire, but, above it all, I could hear with almost startling distinctness the words of the captain, shouting in his clear, high voice, "En avant! Vive la France!"

IV

As we marched forward toward our goal, huge geysers of dust spouted into the air, rising behind our backs from the rows of "75's" supporting us. In front the fire-curtain outlined the whole length of the enemy's line with a neatness and accuracy that struck me with wonder, as the flames burst through the pall of smoke and dust around us. Above, all was blackness, but at its lower edge the curtain was fringed with red and green flames, marking the explosion of the shells directly over the ditch and parapet in front of us. The low-flying clouds mingled with the smoke-curtain, so that the whole brightness of the day was obscured. Out of the blackness fell a trickling rain of pieces of metal, lumps of earth, knapsacks, rifles, cartridges, and fragments of human flesh. We went on steadily, nearer and nearer. Now we seemed very close to the wall of shells streaming from our own guns, curving just above us, and dropping into the trenches in front. The effect was terrific. I almost braced myself against the rocking of the earth, like a sailor's instinctive gait in stormy weather.

In a single spot immediately in front of us, not over ten metres in length, I counted twelve shells bursting so fast that I could not count them without missing other explosions. The scene was horrible and terrifying. Across the wall of our own fire poured shell after shell from the enemy, tearing through our ranks. From overhead the shrapnel seemed to come down in sheets, and from behind the stinking, blinding curtain came volleys of steel-jacketed bullets, their whine unheard and their effect almost unnoticed.

I think we moved forward simply from habit. With me it was like a dream as we went on, ever on. Here and there men dropped, the ranks closing automatically. Of a sudden our own fire-curtain lifted. In a moment it had ceased to bar our way and jumped like a living thing to the next line of the enemy. We could see the trenches in front of us now, quite clear of fire, but flattened almost beyond recognition. The defenders were either killed or demoralized. Calmly, almost stupidly, we parried or thrust with the bayonet at those who barred our way. Without a backward glance we leaped the ditch and went on straight forward toward the next trench, marked in glowing outline by our fire. I remember now how the men looked. Their eyes had a wild, unseeing look in them. Everybody was gazing ahead, trying to pierce the awful curtain which cut us off from all sight of the enemy. Always the black pall smoking and burning appeared ahead—just ahead of us—hiding everything we wanted to see.

The drama was played again and again. Each time, as we approached so close that fragments of our own shells occasionally struck a leading file, the curtain lifted as by magic, jumped the intervening metres, and descended upon the enemy's trench farther on. The ranges were perfect. We followed blindly—sometimes at a walk, sometimes at a dog-trot, and, when close to our goal, on the dead run. You could not hear a word in that pandemonium. All commands were given by example or by gesture. When our captain lay down, we knew our orders were to be down too. When he waved to the right, to the right we swerved; if to the left, we turned to the left. A sweeping gesture, with an arm extended, first up, then down meant, "Halt! Lie down!" From down up, it meant, "Rise!" When his hand was thrust swiftly forward, we knew he was shouting, "En avant!" and when he waved his hand in a circle above his head, we broke into the double-quick.

Three times on our way to the second trench, the captain dropped and we after him. Then three short, quick rushes by the companies and a final dash as the curtain of shells lifted and dropped farther away. Then a hand-to-hand struggle, short and very bloody, some using their bayonets, others clubbing their rifles and grenades. A minute or two, and the trench was ours. The earthen fortress, so strong that the Germans had boasted that it could be held by a janitor and two washerwomen, was in the hands of the Legion.

As we swept on, the trench-cleaners entered the trench behind and began setting things to rights. Far down, six to eight metres below the surface, they found an underground city. Long tunnels, with chambers opening to right and left; bedrooms, furnished with bedsteads, washstands, tables, and chairs; elaborate mess-rooms, some fitted with pianos and phonographs. There were kitchens, too, and even bathrooms. So complex was the labyrinth that three days after the attack Germans were found stowed away in the lateral galleries. The passages were choked with dead. Hundreds of Germans who had survived the bombardment were torn to pieces deep beneath the ground by French hand-grenades, and buried where they lay. In rifles, munitions, and equipment the booty was immense.

We left the subterranean combat raging underneath us and continued on. As we passed over the main trench, we were enfiladed by cannon placed in armored turrets at the end of each section of trench. The danger was formidable, but it, too, had been foreseen. In a few moments these guns were silenced by hand-grenades shoved point-blank through the gun-ports. Just then, I remember, I looked back and saw Pala down on his hands and knees. I turned and ran over to help him up. He was quite dead, killed in the act of rising from the ground. His grotesque posture struck me at the time as funny, and I could not help smiling. I suppose I was nervous.

AMERICANS IN THE FOREIGN LEGION
Showing type of hand-grenades

Our line was wearing thin. Halfway to the third trench we were reinforced by Battalion E coming from behind. The ground in our rear was covered with our men.

All at once came a change. The German artillery in front ceased firing, and the next second we saw the reason why. In the trench ahead, the German troops in black masses were pouring out and advancing toward us at a trot. Was it a counter-attack? "Tant mieux," said a man near me; another, of a different race, said, "We'll show them!" Then as suddenly our own artillery ceased firing, and the mystery became plain. The Germans were approaching in columns of fours, officers to the front, hands held in the air, and, as they came closer, we could distinguish the steady cry, "Kameraden! Kameraden!"

They were surrendering. How we went at our work! Out flew our knives, and, in less time than it takes to tell it, we had mingled among the prisoners, slicing off their trousers buttons, cutting off suspenders, and hacking through belts. All the war shoes had their laces cut, according to the regulations laid down in the last French "Manual," and thus, slopping along, hands helplessly in their breeches pockets to keep their trousers from falling round their ankles, shuffling their feet to keep their boots on, the huge column of prisoners was sent to the rear with a few soldiers to direct rather than to guard them. There was no fight left in them now. A terror-stricken group; some of them, temporarily at least, half insane.

As the Germans left the trenches, their artillery had paused, thinking it a counter-attack. Now, as file after file was escorted to the rear and it became apparent to their rear lines that the men had surrendered, the German artillery saw its mistake and opened up again furiously at the dark masses of defenseless prisoners. We, too, were subjected to a terrific fire. Six shells landed at the same instant in almost the same place, and within a few minutes Section III of our company had almost disappeared. I lost two of my own section, Casey and Leguen, both severely wounded in the leg. I counted fourteen men of my command still on their feet. The company seemed to have shrunk two thirds. A few minutes later, we entered the trench lately evacuated by the Prussians and left it by a very deep communication trench which we knew led to our destination, Ferme Navarin. Just at the entrance we passed signboards, marked in big letters with black paint, SCHÜTZENGRABEN SPANDAU.

This trench ran zigzag, in the general direction north and south. In many places it was filled level with dirt and rocks kicked in by our big shells. From the mass of débris hands and legs were sticking stiffly out at grotesque angles. In one place, the heads of two men showed above the loose brown earth. Here and there, men were sitting, their backs against the wall of the trench, quite dead, with not a wound showing. In one deep crater, excavated by our 320-millimetres, lay five Saxons, side by side, in the pit where they had sought refuge, killed by the bursting of a single shell. One, a man of about twenty-three years of age, lay on his back, his legs tensely doubled, elbows thrust back into the ground, and fingers dug into the palms; eyes staring in terror and mouth wide open. I could not help carrying the picture of fear away with me, and I thought to myself, That man died a coward. Just alongside of him, resting on his left side, lay a blond giant stretched out easily, almost graceful in death. His two hands were laid together, palm to palm, in prayer. Between them was a photograph. The look upon his face was calm and peaceful. The contrast of his figure with his neighbor's struck me. I noticed that a paper protruded from his partly opened blouse, and, picking it up, I read the heading, "Ein' Feste Burg ist Unser Gott." It was a two-leaved tract. I drew a blanket over him and followed my section.

The trench we marched in wound along in the shelter of a little ridge crowned with scrubby pines. Here the German shells bothered us but little. We were out of sight of their observation posts, and, consequently, their fire was uncontrolled and no longer effective. On we went. At every other step our feet pressed down upon soldiers' corpses, lying indiscriminately one on top of the other, sometimes almost filling the trench. I brushed against one who sat braced against the side of the trench, the chin resting upon folded arms naturally—yet quite dead. It was through this trench that the Germans had tried to rush reinforcements into the threatened position, and here the men were slaughtered, without a chance to go back or forward. Hemmed in by shells in both front and rear, many hundreds had climbed into the open and tried to escape over the fields toward the pine forest, only to be mown down as they ran. For hundreds of metres continuously my feet, as I trudged along, did not touch the ground. In many of the bodies life was not yet extinct, but we had to leave them for the Red Cross men. We had our orders. No delay was possible, and, at any rate, our minds were clogged with our own work ahead.

Making such time as we could, we finally arrived at the summit of the little ridge. Then we left the cover of the trench, formed in Indian file, fifty metres between sections, and, at the signal, moved forward swiftly and in order.

It was a pretty bit of tactics and executed with a dispatch and neatness hardly equalled on the drill-ground. The first files of the sections were abreast, while the men fell in, one close behind the other; and so we crossed the ridge, offering the smallest possible target to the enemy's guns. Before us and a little to our left was the Ferme Navarin, our goal. As we descended the slope, we were greeted by a new hail of iron. Shells upon shells, fired singly, by pairs, by salvos, from six-gun batteries, crashed and exploded around us.

We increased the pace to a run and arrived out of breath abreast of immense pits dynamited out of the ground by prodigious explosions. Embedded in them we could see three enemy howitzers, but not a living German was left. All had disappeared.

We entered the pits and rested for a space. After a moment we crawled up the side of the pit and peeked over the edge. There I could see Doumergue stretched on the ground. He was lying on his back, his shoulders and head supported by his knapsack. His right leg was doubled under him, and I could see that he had been struck down in the act of running. As I watched, he strained weakly to roll himself sideways and free his leg. Slowly, spasmodically, his leg moved. Very, very slowly the foot dragged itself along the ground, and finally the limb was stretched alongside the other. Then I saw his rough, wan face assume a look of satisfaction. His eyes closed. A sigh passed between his lips, and Doumergue had gone with the rest.

As we waited there, the mood of the men seemed to change. Their spirits began to rise. One jest started another, and soon we were all laughing at the memory of the German prisoners marching to the rear, holding up their trousers with both hands. Some of the men had taken the welcome opportunity of searching the prisoners while cutting their suspenders, and most of them were now puffing German cigarettes. One of them, Haeffle, offered me a piece of K.K. bread,1 black as ink. I declined with thanks, for I didn't like the looks of it. In the relaxation of the moment, nobody paid any attention to the shells falling outside the little open shelter, until Capdeveille proposed to crawl inside one of the German howitzers for security. Alas, he was too fat, and stuck! I myself hoped rather strongly that no shell would enter one of these pits in which the company had found shelter, because I knew there were several thousand rounds of ammunition piled near each piece hidden under the dirt, and an explosion might make it hot for us.

As we sat there, smoking and chatting, Delpeuch, the *homme des liaisons*, as he is called, of the company, slid over the edge of the hollow and brought with him the order to leave the pit in single file and to descend to the bottom of the incline, in line with some trees which he pointed out to us. There we were to deploy in open order and dig shelter-trenches for ourselves—though I can tell the reader that "shelter" is a poor word to use in such a connection. It seems we had to wait for artillery before making the attack on Navarin itself. The trench "Spandau," so Delpeuch told me, was being put into shape by the engineers and was already partially filled with troops who were coming up to our support. The same message had been carried to the other section. As we filed out of our pit, we saw them leaving theirs. In somewhat loose formation, we ran full-tilt down the hill, and, at the assigned position, flung ourselves on the ground and began digging like mad. We had made the last stretch without losing a man.

The Ferme Navarin was two hundred metres from where we lay. From it came a heavy rifle and mitrailleuse fire, but we did not respond. We had something else to do. Every man had his shovel, and every man made the dirt fly. In what seemed half a minute we had formed a continuous parapet, twelve to fourteen inches in height, and with our knapsacks placed to keep the dirt in position, we felt quite safe against infantry and machine-gun fire. Next, each man proceeded to dig his little individual niche in the ground, about a yard deep, twenty inches wide, and long enough to lie down in with comfort. Between each two men there remained a partition wall of dirt, from ten to fifteen inches thick, the usefulness of which was immediately demonstrated by a shell which fell into Blondino's niche, blowing him to pieces without injuring either of his companions to the right or the left.

We were comfortable and able to take pot shots at the Germans and to indulge again in the old trench game of sticking a helmet on a bayonet, pushing it a little above the dirt, and thus coaxing the Germans into a shot and immediately responding with four or five rifles. I looked at my watch. It said 10.45—just an hour and a half since we had left our trenches and started on our charge; an hour and a half in which I had lived days and years.

I was pretty well tired out and would have given the world for a few hours' sleep. I called to Merrick to toss me Blondino's canteen. Mine was empty, and Blondino had left his behind when he departed with the 105-millimetre. Haeffle remarked that Blondino was always making a noise anyway.

The artillery fire died down gradually and only one German battery was still sweeping us now. Our long-range pieces thundered behind us, and we could hear shells "swooshing" overhead in a constant stream on their way to the German target. Our fire was evidently beating down the German artillery fire excepting the single battery which devoted its attention to us. The guns were hidden, and our artillery did not seem able to locate them. Our aeroplanes, long hovering overhead, began to swoop dangerously low. A swift Morane plane swept by at a height of two hundred metres over the pine forest where the German guns were hidden. We watched him as he returned safe to our lines.

Soon the order came down the line to deepen the trenches. It seemed we were to stay there until night.

The charge was over.

1

Kriegs Kartoffel Brot.

V

Time passed very slowly. I raised my arm to listen to my wrist-watch, but couldn't hear it. Too many shells!

I knelt cautiously in my hole, and, looking over the edge, counted my section. There were but eighteen men. The Collettes, both corporals, were on the extreme left. Next came Capdeveille, Dowd, Zinn, Seeger, Scanlon, King, Soubiron, Dubois, Corporal Mettayer, Haeffle, Saint-Hilaire, Schneli, De Sumera, Corporal Denis, Bur-bekkar, and Birchler. On my left, two paces in the rear of the section, were Neumayer, Corporal Fourrier, and Sergeant Fourrier. Both these were supernumeraries. The second sergeant was over with Section II. I began now to realize our losses. Fully two thirds of my section were killed or wounded.

I wanted information from Corporal Denis regarding the men of his squad. Throwing a lump of dirt at him to attract his attention, I motioned to him to roll over to the side of his hole and make a place for me. Then, with two quick jumps I landed alongside him. As I dropped we noticed spurts of dust rising from the dirt-pile in front of the hole and smiled. The Germans were too slow that time. Putting my lips to his ears, I shouted my questions and got my information.

This hole was quite large enough to accommodate both of us, so I decided to stay with him awhile. Corporal Denis still had bread and cheese and shared it with me. We lunched in comfort.

Having finished, we rolled cigarettes. I had no matches, and as he reached his cigarette to me to light mine, he jumped almost to his feet, rolled on his face, and with both hands clasped to his face, tried to rise, but couldn't. I've seen men who were knocked out in the squared ring do the same thing. With heads resting on the floor, they try to get up. They get up on their knees and seem to try to lift their heads, but can't. Denis tugged and tugged, without avail. I knelt alongside him and forced his hands from his face. He was covered with blood spurting out of a three-inch gash running from the left eye down to the corner of the mouth. A steel splinter had entered there and passed under the left ear. He must stay in the trench until nightfall.

I reached for his emergency dressing and as I made the motion felt a blow in the right shoulder. As soon as I had got Denis tied up and quiet, I unbuttoned my coat and shirt and picked a rifle-ball out of my own shoulder. The wound was not at all serious and bled but little. I congratulated myself, but wondered why the ball did not penetrate; and then I caught sight of Denis's rifle lying over the parapet and showing a hole in the woodwork. The ball seemed to have passed through the magazine of the rifle, knocked out one cartridge, and then hit me.

When I was ready to return to my own hole, I rose a little too high and the Germans turned loose with a machine gun, but too high. I got back safely and lay down. It was getting very monotonous. To pass the time, I dug my hole deeper and larger, placing the loose dirt in front in a quarter-circle, until I felt perfectly safe against anything except a direct hit by a shell. There is but one chance in a thousand of that happening.

The day passed slowly and without mishap to my section. As night fell, one half of the section stayed on the alert four hours, while the other half slept. The second sergeant had returned and relieved me at twelve, midnight. I pulled several handfuls of grass, and with that and two overcoats I had stripped from dead Germans during the night, I made a comfortable bed and lay down to sleep. The bank was not uncomfortable. I was very tired, and dozed off immediately.

Suddenly I awoke in darkness. Everything was still, and I could hear my watch ticking, but over every part of me there was an immense leaden weight. I tried to rise, and couldn't move. Something was holding me and choking me at the same time. There was no air to breathe. I set my muscles and tried to give a strong heave. As I drew in my breath, my mouth filled with dirt. I was buried alive!

It is curious what a man thinks about when he is in trouble. Into my mind shot memories of feats of strength performed. Why, I was the strongest man in the section. Surely I could lift myself out, I thought to myself, and my confidence began to return. I worked the dirt out of my mouth with the tip of my tongue and prepared myself mentally for the sudden heave that would free me. A quick inhalation, and my mouth filled again with dirt. I could not move a muscle under my skin. And then I seemed to be two people. The "I" who was thinking seemed to be at a distance from the body lying there.

My God! Am I going to die stretched out in a hole like this? I thought.

Through my mind flashed a picture of the way I had always hoped to die— the way I had a right to die: face to the enemy and running toward him. Why, that was part of a soldier's wages. I tried to shout for help, and more dirt entered my mouth! I could feel it gritting way down in my throat. My tongue was locked so I could not move it. I watched the whole picture. I was standing a little way off and could hear myself gurgle. My throat was rattling, and I said to myself, "That's the finish!" Then I grew calm. It wasn't hurting so much, and somehow or other I seemed to realize that a soldier had taken a soldier's chance and lost. It wasn't his fault. He had done the best he could. Then the pain all left me and the world went black. It was death.

Then somebody yelled, "Hell! He bit my finger." I could hear him.

"That's nothing," said a voice I knew as Collette's. "Get the dirt out of his mouth."

Again a finger entered my throat, and I coughed spasmodically.

Some one was working my arms backward, and my right shoulder hurt me. I struggled up, but sank to my knees and began coughing up dirt.

"Here," says Soubiron, "turn round and spit that dirt on your parapet. It all helps." The remark made me smile.

I was quite all right now, and Soubiron, Collette, Joe, and Marcel returned to their holes. The Red Cross men were picking something out of the hole made by a 250-millimetre, they told me. It was the remnant of Corporal and Sergeant Fourrier, who had their trench to my left. It seems that a ten-inch shell had entered the ground at the edge of my hole, exploded a depth of two metres, tearing the corporal and the sergeant to pieces, and kicking several cubic metres of dirt into and on top of me. Soubiron and the Collettes saw what had happened, and immediately started digging me out. They had been just in time. It wasn't long before my strength began to come back. Two stretcher-bearers came up to carry me to the rear, but I declined their services. There was too much going on. I dug out the German overcoats, recovered some grass, and, bedding myself down in the crater made by the shell, began to feel quite safe again. Lightning never strikes twice in the same spot.

However, that wasn't much like the old-fashioned lightning. The enemy seemed to have picked upon my section. The shells were falling thicker and closer. Everybody was broad awake now, and all of us seemed to be waiting for a shell to drop into our holes. It was only a question of time before we should be wiped out. Haeffle called my attention to a little trench we all had noticed during the daytime, about forty metres in front of us. No fire had come from there, and it was evidently quite abandoned.

I took Haeffle and Saint-Hilaire with me and quietly crawled over to the trench, round the end of it, and started to enter at about the middle.

Then all of a sudden a wild yell came out of the darkness in front of us.

"Franzosen! Die Franzosen!"

We couldn't see anything, nor they either. There might have been a regiment of us, or of them for that matter. I screeched out in German,

"Hände hoch!" and jumped into the trench followed by my two companions. As we crouched in the bottom, I yelled again, "Hände hoch oder wir schiessen!"

The response was the familiar "Kameraden! Kameraden!" Haeffle gave an audible chuckle.

Calling again on my German, I ordered the men to step out of the trench with hands held high, and to march toward our line. I assured the poor devils we wouldn't hurt them. They thought there was a division of us, more or less, and I don't know how much confidence they put in my assurance. Anyhow, as they scrambled over the parapet, I counted six of them prisoners to the three of us. Haeffle and Saint-Hilaire escorted them back and also took word to the second sergeant to let the section crawl, one after the other, up this trench to where I was.

One by one the men came on, crawling in single file, and I put them to work, carefully and noiselessly reversing the parapet. This German trench was very deep, with niches cut into the bank at intervals of one metre, permitting the men to lie down comfortably.

It was then that I happened to feel of my belt. One of the straps had been cut clean through and my wallet, which had held two hundred and sixty-five francs, had been neatly removed. Some one of my men, who had risked his life for mine with a self-devotion that could scarcely be surpassed, had felt that his need was greater than mine. Whoever he was, I bear him no grudge. Poor chap, if he lived he needed the money—and that day he surely did me a good turn. Besides, he was a member of the Legion.

I placed sentries, took care to find a good place for myself, and was just dropping off to sleep as Haeffle and Saint-Hilaire returned and communicated to me the captain's compliments and the assurance of a "*citation*."

I composed myself to sleep and dropped off quite content.

VI

It seemed but a few minutes when I was awakened by Collette and Marcel, who offered me a steaming cup of coffee, half a loaf of bread, and some Swiss cheese. This food had been brought from the rear while I was lying asleep. My appetite was splendid, and when Sergeant Malvoisin offered me a drink of rum in a canteen that he took off a dead German, I accepted gratefully. Just then the *agent de liaison* appeared, with the order to assemble the section, and in single file, second section at thirty-metre interval, to return the way we had come.

It was almost daylight and things were visible at two to three metres. The bombardment had died down and the quiet was hardly disturbed by occasional shots. Our captain marched ahead of the second section, swinging a cane and contentedly puffing on his pipe. Nearly everybody was smoking. As we marched along we noticed that new trenches had been dug during the night, from sixty to a hundred metres in the rear of the position we had held, and these trenches were filled by the Twenty-ninth Chasseurs Regiment, which replaced us.

Very cunningly these trenches were arranged. They were deep and narrow, fully seven feet deep and barely a yard wide. At every favorable point, on every little rise in the ground, a salient had been constructed, projecting out from the main trench ten to fifteen metres, protected by heavy logs, corrugated steel sheets, and two to three feet of dirt. Each side of the salients bristled with machine guns. Any attack upon this position would be bound to fail, owing to the intense volume of fire that could be brought to bear upon the flanks of the enemy.

To make assurance doubly sure, the Engineer Corps had dug rows of cup-shaped bowls, two feet in diameter, two feet deep, leaving but a narrow wedge of dirt between each two; and in the center of each bowl was placed a six-pointed twisted steel "porcupine." This instrument, no matter how placed, always presents a sharp point right at you. Five rows of these man-traps I counted, separated by a thin wall of dirt, not strong enough to maintain the weight of a man, so that any one who attempted to rush past would be thrown against the "porcupine" and be spitted like a pigeon. As an additional precaution a mass of barbed wire lay in rolls, ready to be placed in front of this *ouvrage*, to make it safe against any surprise.

We marched along, talking and chatting, discussing this and that, without a care in the world. Every one hoped we were going to the rear to recuperate and enjoy a good square meal and a good night's rest. Seeger wanted a good wash, he said. He was rather dirty, and so was I. My puttees dangled in pieces round my calves. It seems I had torn them going through the German wire the day before. I told Haeffle to keep his eyes open for a good pair on some dead man. He said he would.

The company marched round the hill we descended so swiftly yesterday and, describing a semicircle, entered again the *Schützengraben Spandau* and marched back in the direction we had come from. The trench, however, presented a different appearance. The bad places had been repaired, the loose dirt had been shoveled out, and the dead had disappeared. On the east side of the trench an extremely high parapet had been built. In this parapet even loopholes appeared—rather funny-looking loopholes, I thought; and when I looked closer, I saw that they were framed in by boots! I reached my hand into several of them as we walked along, and touched the limbs of dead men. The engineer, it seems, in need of material, had placed the dead Germans on top of the ground, feet flush with the inside of the ditch, leaving from six to seven inches between two bodies, and laying another body crosswise on top of the two, spanning the gap between them. Then they had shoveled the dirt on top of them, thus killing two birds with one stone.

The discovery created a riot of excitement among the men. Curses intermingled with laughter came from ahead of us. Everybody was tickled by the ingenuity of our *génie*. "They are marvelous!" we thought. Dowd's face showed consternation, yet he could not help smiling. Little King was pale around the mouth, yet his lips were twisted in a grin. It was horribly amusing.

Every two hundred metres we passed groups of soldiers of the one Hundred and Seventieth Regiment on duty in the trench. The front line, they told us, was twelve hundred metres farther east, and this trench formed the second line for their regiment. We entered the third-line trench of the Germans, from which they ran yesterday to surrender, and continued marching in the same direction—always east. Here we had a chance to investigate the erstwhile German habitations.

Exactly forty paces apart doorways opened into the dirt bank, and from each of them fourteen steps descended at about forty-five degrees into a cellar-like room. The stairs were built of wood and the sides of the stairways and the chambers below were lined with one-inch pine boards. These domiciles must have been quite comfortable and safe, but now they were choked with bodies. As we continued our leisurely way, we met some of our trench-cleaners and they recited their experiences with gusto. The Germans, they told us, pointing down into the charnel-houses, refused to come and give up, and even fired at them when summoned to surrender.

"Then what did you do?" I asked. "Very simple," answered one. "We stood on the top of the ground right above the door and hurled grenade after grenade through the doorway until all noise gradually ceased down below. Then we went to the next hole and did the same thing. It wasn't at all dangerous," he added, "and very effective."

We moved but slowly along the trench, and every once in a while there was a halt while some of the men investigated promising "prospects," where the holes packed with dead Germans held out some promise of loot. Owing to the order of march, the first company was the last one in line, and my section at the very end. The head of the column was the fourth company, then the third, the second; and then we. By the time my section came to any hole holding out hopes of souvenirs, there was nothing left for us. Yet I did find a German officer with a new pair of leg-bands, and, hastily unwinding them, I discarded my own and put on the new ones. As I bound them on I noticed the name on the tag—"Hindenburg." I suppose the name stands for quality with the Boches.

We left the trench and swung into another communication trench, going to the left, still in an easterly direction, straight on toward the Butte de Souain. That point we knew was still in the hands of the Germans, and very quickly they welcomed us. Shells came shrieking down—one hundred and five millimetres, one hundred and fifty, two hundred and ten, and two hundred and fifty. It's very easy to tell when you are close to them, even though you can't see a thing. When a big shell passes high, it sounds like a white-hot piece of iron suddenly doused in cold water; but when it gets close, the *sw-i-ish* suddenly rises in a high crescendo, a shriek punctuated by a horrible roar. The uniformity of movement as the men ducked was beautiful!—and they all did it. One moment there was a line of gray helmets bobbing up and down the trenches as the line plodded on; and the next instant one could see only a line of black canvas close to the ground, as every man ducked and shifted his shoulder-sack over his neck. My sack had been blown to pieces when I was buried, and I felt uncomfortably handicapped with only my *musette* for protection against steel splinters.

About a mile from where we entered this *boyau*, we came to a temporary halt, then went on once more. The fourth company had come to a halt, and we squeezed past them as we marched along. Every man of them had his shovel out and had commenced digging a niche for himself. We passed the fourth company, then the third, then the second, and finally the first, second, and third sections of our own company. Just beyond, we ourselves came to a halt and, lining up one man per metre, started to organize the trench for defensive purposes. From the other side of a slight ridge, east of us, and about six hundred metres away, came the sound of machine guns. Between us and the ridge the Germans were executing a very lively *feu de barrage*, a screen of fire, prohibiting any idea of sending reinforcements over to the front line.

Attached for rations to my section were the commandant of the battalion, a captain, and three sergeants of the État-Major. Two of the sergeants were at the trench telephone, and I could hear them report the news to the officers. "The Germans," they reported, "are penned in on three sides and are prevented from retreating by our artillery." Twice they had tried to pierce our line between them and the Butte de Souain, and twice they were driven back. Good news for us!

At 10 A.M. we sent three men from each section to the rear for the soup. At about eleven they reappeared with steaming *marmites* of soup, stew, and coffee, and buckets of wine. The food was very good, and disappeared to the last morsel.

After we had eaten, the captain granted me permission to walk along the ditch back to the fourth company. The trench being too crowded for comfort, I walked alongside to the second company, and searched for my friend Sergeant Velte. Finally I found him lying in a shell-hole, side by side with his adjutant and Sergeant Morin. All three were dead, torn to pieces by one shell shortly after we had passed them in the morning. At the third company they reported that Second Lieutenant Sweeny had been shot through the chest by a lost ball that morning. Hard luck for Sweeny![2] The poor devil had just been nominated *sous-lieutenant* at the request of the French Embassy in Washington, and when he was attached as supernumerary to the third company we all had hopes that he would have a chance to prove his merit.

In the fourth company also the losses were severe. The part of the trench occupied by the three companies was directly enfiladed by the German batteries on the Butte de Souain, and every little while a shell would fall square into the ditch and take toll from the occupants. Our company was fully a thousand metres nearer to these batteries, but the trenches we occupied presented a three-quarters face to the fire, and consequently were ever so much harder to hit. Even then, when I got back I found four men *hors de combat* in the fourth section. In my section two niches were demolished without any one being hit.

Time dragged slowly until four in the afternoon, when we had soup again. Many of the men built little fires and with the *Erbsenwurst* they had found on dead Germans prepared a very palatable soup by way of extra rations.

At four o'clock sentries were posted and everybody fell asleep. A steady rain was falling, and to keep dry we hooked one edge of our tent-sheet on the ground above the niche and placed dirt on top of it to hold. Then we pushed cartridges through the button-holes of the tent, pinning them into the side of the trench and forming a good cover for the occupant of the hole. Thus we rested until the new day broke, bringing a clear sky and sunshine. This day, the 27th,—the third of the battle,—passed without mishap to my section. We spent our time eating and sleeping, mildly distracted by an intermittent bombardment.

2

Lieutenant Sweeny has returned to America.

VII

Another night spent in the same cramped quarters! We were getting weary of inactivity, and it was rather hard work to keep the men in the ditch. They sneaked off singly and in pairs, always heading back to the German dugouts, all bent on turning things upside down in the hope of finding something of value to carry as a keepsake.

Haeffle came back once with three automatic pistols but no cartridges. From another trip he returned with an officer's helmet, and the third time he brought triumphantly back a string three feet long of dried sausages. Haeffle always did have a healthy appetite and it transpired that on the way back he had eaten a dozen sausages, more or less. The dried meat had made him thirsty and he had drunk half a canteen of water on top of it. The result was, he swelled up like a poisoned pup, and for a time he was surely a sick man.

Zinn found two shiny German bayonets, a long thin one and one short and heavy, and swore he'd carry them for a year if he had to. Zinn hailed from Battle Creek and wanted to use them as brush-knives on camping trips in the Michigan woods; but alas, in the sequel they got too heavy and were dropped along the road. One man found a German pipe with a three-foot soft-rubber stem, which he intended sending to his brother as a souvenir. Man and pipe are buried on the slopes of the Butte de Souain. He died that same evening.

At the usual time, 4 P.M., we had soup, and immediately after came the order to get ready. Looking over the trench, we watched the fourth company form in the open back of the ditch and, marching past us in an oblique direction, disappear round a spur of wooded hill. The third company followed at four hundred metres' distance, then the second, and as they passed out of sight around the hill, we jumped out and, forming in line, sections at thirty-metre intervals, each company four hundred metres in the rear of the one ahead, we followed, *arme à la bretelle*.

We were quite unobserved by the enemy, and marched the length of the hill for three fourths of a kilometre, keeping just below the crest. Above us sailed four big French battle-planes and some small aero scouts, on the lookout for enemy aircraft. For a while it seemed as if we should not be discovered, and the command was given to lie down. From where we lay we could observe clearly the ensuing scrap in the air, and it was worth watching. Several German planes had approached close to our lines, but were discovered by the swift-flying scouts. Immediately the little fellows returned with the news to the big planes, and we watched the monster biplanes mount to the combat. In a wide circle they swung, climbing, climbing higher and higher, and then headed in a beeline straight toward the German *tauben*. As they approached within range of each other, we saw little clouds appear close to the German planes, some in front, some over them, and others behind; and then, after an interval, the report of the thirty-two-millimetre guns mounted on our battle-planes floated down to us, immediately followed like an echo by the crack of the bursting shell. Long before the Germans could get within effective range for their machine guns, they were peppered by our planes and ignominiously forced to beat a retreat. One "albatross" seemed to be hit. He staggered from one side to the other, then dipped forward, and, standing straight on his nose, dropped like a stone out of sight behind the forest crowning the hill.

Again we moved on, and shortly arrived at the southern spur of the hill. Here the company made a quarter turn to the left, and in the same formation began the ascent of the hill. The second company was just disappearing into the scrubby pine forest on top. We entered also, continued on to the top, and halted just below the crest. The captain called the officers and sergeants and, following him, we crawled on our stomachs up to the highest point and looked over.

Never shall I forget the panorama that spread before us! The four thin ranks of the second company seemed to stagger drunkenly through a sea of green fire and smoke. One moment gaps showed in the lines, only to be closed again as the rear files spurted. Undoubtedly they ran at top speed, but to us watchers they seemed to crawl, and at times almost to stop. Mixed in with the dark green of the grass covering the valley were rows of lighter color, telling of the men who fell in that mad sprint. The continuous bombardment sounded like a giant drum beating an incredibly swift *rataplan*. Along the whole length of our hill this curtain of shells was dropping, leveling the forest and seemingly beating off the very face of the hill itself, clean down to the bottom of the valley. Owing to the proximity of our troops to the enemy's batteries we received hardly any support from our own big guns, and the rôle of the combatants was entirely reversed. The Germans had their innings then and full well they worked.

As the company descended into the valley the pace became slower, and at the beginning of the opposite slope they halted and faced back. Owing to the height of the Butte de Souain, they were safe, and they considered that it was their turn to act as spectators.

As our captain rose we followed and took our places in front of our sections. Again I impressed upon the minds of my men the importance of following in a straight line and as close behind one another as possible.

"Arme à la main!" came the order, and slowly we moved to the crest and then immediately broke into a dog-trot. Instantly we were enveloped in flames and smoke. Hell kissed us welcome! Closely I watched the captain for the sign to increase our speed. I could have run a mile in record time, but he plugged steadily along, one, two, three, four, one, two, three, four, at a tempo of a hundred and eighty steps per minute, three to the second,— the regulation tempo. Inwardly I cursed his insistence upon having things *réglementaires*.

As I looked at the middle of his back, longing for him to hurry, I caught sight, on my right, of a shell exploding directly in the center of the third section. Out of the tail of my eye I saw the upper part of Corporal Keraudy's body rise slowly into the air. The legs had disappeared, and with arms outstretched the trunk sank down upon the corpse of Varma, the Hindu, who had marched behind him. Instinctively, I almost stopped in my tracks—Keraudy was a friend of mine—but at the instant Corporal Mettayer, running behind me, bumped into my back, and shoved me again into life and action.

We were out of the woods then, and running down the bare slope of the hill. A puff of smoke, red-hot, smote me in the face, and at the same moment intense pain shot up my jaw. I did not think I was hit seriously, since I was able to run all right. Some one in the second section intoned the regimental march, "Allons, Giron." Others took it up; and there in that scene of death and hell, this song portraying the lusts and vices of the Légion Étrangère became a very pæan of enthusiasm and courage.

Glancing to the right, I saw that we were getting too close to the second section, so I gave the signal for a left oblique. We bore away from them until once again at our thirty paces' distance. All at once my feet tangled up in something and I almost fell. It was long grass! Just then it seemed to grow upon my mind that we were down in the valley and out of range of the enemy. Then I glanced ahead, and not over a hundred metres away I saw the second company lying in the grass and watching us coming. As we neared, they shouted little pleasantries at us and congratulated us upon our speed.

"Why this unseemly haste?" one wants to know.

"You go to the devil!" answers Haeffle.

"Merci, mon ami!" retorts the first; "I have just come through his back kitchen."

Counting my section, I missed Dubois, Saint-Hilaire, and Schneli. Collette, Joe told me, was left on the hill.

The company had lost two sergeants, one corporal, and thirteen men, coming down that short stretch! We mustered but forty-five men, all told. One, Sergeant Terisien, had for four months commanded my section, the "American Section," but was transferred to the fourth section. From where we rested we could see him slowly descending the hill, bareheaded and with his right hand clasping his left shoulder. He had been severely wounded in the head, and his left arm was nearly torn off at the shoulder. Poor devil! He was a good comrade and a good soldier. Just before the war broke out he had finished his third enlistment in the Legion, and was in line for a discharge and pension when he died.

Looking up the awful slope we had just descended, we could see the bodies of our comrades, torn and mangled and again and again kicked up into the air by the shells. For two days and nights the hellish hail continued to beat upon that blood-soaked slope, until we finally captured the Butte de Souain and forced an entire regiment of Saxons to the left of the butte to capitulate.

Again we assembled in column of fours, and this time began the climb uphill. Just then I happened to think of the blow I had received under the jaw, and feeling of the spot, discovered a slight wound under my left jawbone. Handing my rifle to a man, I pressed slightly upon the sore spot and pulled a steel splinter out of the wound. A very thin, long sliver of steel it was, half the diameter of a dime and not more than a dime's thickness, but an inch and a half long. The metal was still hot to the touch. The scratch continued bleeding freely, and I did not bandage it at the time because I felt sure of needing my emergency dressing farther along.

Up near the crest of the hill we halted in an angle of the woods and lay down alongside the One Hundred and Seventy-second Regiment of infantry. They had made the attack in this direction on the twenty-fifth, but had been severely checked at this point. Infantry and machine-gun fire sounded very close, and lost bullets by the hundreds flicked through the branches overhead. The One Hundred and Seventy-second informed us that a battalion of the Premier Étranger had entered the forest and was at that moment storming a position to our immediate left. Through the trees showed lights, brighter than day, cast from hundreds of German magnesium candles shot into the air.

Our officers were grouped with those of the other regiment, and after a very long conference they separated, each to his command. Our captain called the officers and subalterns of the company together, and in terse sentences explained to us our positions and the object of the coming assault. It was to be a purely local affair, it seemed, and the point was the clearing of the enemy from the hill we were on. On a map drawn to scale he pointed out the lay of the land.

It looked to me like a hard proposition. Imagine to yourself a toothbrush about a mile long and three eighths to one half mile wide. The back is formed by the summit of the hill, densely wooded, and the bristles are represented by four little ridges rising from the valley we had just crossed, each one crowned with strips of forest and uniting with the main ridges at right angles. Between each two lines of bristles are open spaces, from one hundred to one hundred and fifty metres wide. We of the second regiment were to deliver the assault parallel with the bristles and stretching from the crest down to the valley.

The other column was to make a demonstration from our left, running a general course at right angles to ours. The time set was eight o'clock at night.

Returning to our places, we informed the men of what they were in for. While we were talking we noticed a group of men come from the edge of the woods and form into company formation, and we could hear them answer to the roll-call. I went over and peered at them. On their coat-collars I saw the gilt "No. 1." It was the Premier Étranger.

As the roll-call proceeded, I wondered. The sergeant was deciphering with difficulty the names from his little *carnet*, and response after response was, "Mort." Once in a while the answer changed to, "Mort sur le champ d'honneur," or a brief "Tombé." There were twenty-two men in line, not counting the sergeant and a corporal, who in rear of the line supported himself precariously on two rifles which served him as crutches. Two more groups appeared back of this one, and the same proceeding was repeated. As I stood near the second group I could just catch the responses of the survivors. "Duvivier": "Présent."—"Selonti": "Présent."—"Boismort": "Tombé."—"Herkis": "Mort."—"Carney": "Mort."—"MacDonald": "Présent."—"Farnsworth": "Mort sur le champ d'honneur," responded MacDonald. Several of the men I had known, Farnsworth among them. One officer, a second-lieutenant, commanded the remains of the battalion. Seven hundred and fifty men, he informed me, had gone in an hour ago, and less than two hundred came back.

AMERICANS IN THE FOREIGN LEGION RECEIVING NEWS
FROM HOME

"Ah, mon ami," he told me, "c'est bien chaud dans le bois."

Quietly they turned into column of fours and disappeared in the darkness. Their attack had failed. Owing to the protection afforded by the trees, our aerial scouts had failed to gather definite information of the defenses constructed in the forest, and owing also to the same cause, our previous bombardment had been ineffective.

It was our job to remedy this. One battalion of the One Hundred and Seventy-second was detached and placed in line with us, and at 8 P.M. sharp the commandant's whistle sounded, echoed by that of our captain.

Quietly we lined up at the edge of the forest, shoulder to shoulder, bayonets fixed. Quietly each corporal examined the rifles of his men, inspected the magazines, and saw that each chamber also held a cartridge with firing-pin down. As silently as possible we entered between the trees and carefully kept in touch with each other. It was dark in there, and we had moved along some little distance before our eyes were used to the blackness. As I picked my steps I prepared myself for the shock every man experiences at the first sound of a volley. Twice I fell down into shell-holes and cursed my clumsiness and that of some other fellows to my right. "The 'Dutch' must be asleep," I thought, "or else they beat it." Hopefully, the latter!

We were approaching the farther edge of the "toothbrush bristles," and breathlessly we halted at the edge of the little open space before us. About eighty metres across loomed the black line of another "row of bristles." I wondered.

The captain and second section to our right moved on and we kept in line, still slowly and cautiously, carefully putting one foot before the other. Suddenly from the darkness in front of us came four or five heavy reports like the noise of a shotgun, followed by a long hiss. Into the air streamed trails of sparks. Above our heads the hiss ended with a sharp crack, and everything stood revealed as though it were broad daylight.

At the first crash, the major, the captains—everybody, it seemed to me—yelled at the same time, "En avant! Pas de charge!"—and in full run, with fixed bayonets, we flew across the meadow. As we neared the woods we were met by solid sheets of steel balls. Roar upon roar came from the forest; the volleys came too fast, it shot into my mind, to be well aimed. Then something hit me on the chest and I fell sprawling. Barbed wire! Everybody seemed to be on the ground at once, crawling, pushing, struggling through. My rifle was lost and I grasped my *parabellum*. It was a German weapon, German charges, German cartridges. This time the Germans were to get a taste of their own medicine, I thought. Lying on my back, I wormed through the wire, butting into the men in front of me and getting kicked in the head by Mettayer. As I crawled I could hear the *ping*, *ping*, of balls striking the wire, and the shrill moan as they glanced off and continued on their flight.

Putting out my hand, I felt loose dirt, and, lying flat, peered over the parapet. "Nobody home," I thought; and then I saw one of the Collette brothers in the trench come running toward me and ahead of him a burly Boche. I saw Joe make a one-handed lunge with the rifle, and saw the bayonet show fully a foot in front of the German's chest.

Re-forming, we advanced toward the farther fringe of the little forest. Half-way through the trees we lay down flat on our stomachs, rifle in right hand, and slowly, very slowly, wormed our way past the trees into the opening between us and our goal. Every man had left his knapsack in front or else hanging on the barbed wire, and we were in good shape for the work that lay ahead. But the sections and companies were inextricably mixed. On one side of me crawled a lieutenant of the One Hundred and Seventy-second, and on the other a private I had never seen before. Still we were all in line, and when some one shouted, "Feu de quatre cartouches!" we fired four rounds, and after the command all crawled again a few paces nearer.

Several times we halted to fire, aiming at the sheets of flame spurting toward us. Over the Germans floated several parachute magnesium rockets, sent up by our own men, giving a vivid light and enabling us to shoot with fair accuracy. I think now that the German fire was too high. Anyway, I did not notice any one in my immediate vicinity getting hit. Though our progress was slow, we finally arrived at the main wire entanglement.

All corporals in the French army carry wire-nippers, and it was our corporal's business to open a way through the entanglement. Several men to my right, I could see one,—he looked like Mettayer,—lying flat on his back and, nippers in hand, snipping away at the wire overhead, while all of us behind kept up a murderous and constant fire at the enemy. Mingled with the roar of the rifles came the stuttering rattle of the machine guns, at moments drowned by the crash of hand-grenades. Our grenadiers had rather poor success with their missiles, however, most of them hitting trees in front of the trench. The lieutenant on my left had four grenades. I could see him plainly. With one in his hand, he crawled close to the wire, rolled on his back, rested an instant with arms extended, both hands grasping the grenade, then suddenly he doubled forward and back and sent the bomb flying over his head. For two—three seconds,—it seemed longer at the time,—we listened, and then came the roar of the explosion. He smiled and nodded to me, and again went through the same manœuvre.

In the mean time I kept my *parabellum* going. I had nine magazines loaded with dum-dum balls I had taken from some dead Germans, and I distributed the balls impartially between three *créneaux* in front of me. On my right, men were surging through several breaks in the wire. Swiftly I rolled over and over toward the free lane and went through with a rush. The combat had degenerated into a hand-grenade affair. Our grenadiers crawled alongside the parapet and every so often tossed one of their missiles into it, while the others, shooting over their heads, potted the Germans as they ran to rear.

Suddenly the fusillade ceased, and with a crash, it seemed, silence and darkness descended upon us. The sudden cessation of the terrific rifle firing and of the constant rattling of the machine guns struck one like a blow. Sergeant Altoffer brought me some information about one of my men, and almost angrily I asked him not to shout! "I'm not deaf yet," I assured him. "Mon vieux," he raged, "it's you who are shouting!"

I realized my fault and apologized and in return accepted a drink of wine from his canteen.

Finding the captain, we received the order to assemble the men and maintain the trench, and after much searching I found a few men of the section. The little scrap had cost the first section three more men. Soubiron, Dowd, and Zinn were wounded and sent to the rear. The One Hundred and Seventy-second sent a patrol toward the farthest, the last, bristle of the toothbrush, with the order to reconnoiter thoroughly. An hour passed and they had not returned. Twenty minutes more went by and still no patrol. Rather curious, we thought. No rifle-shots had come from that direction nor any noise such as would be heard during a combat with the bayonet. The commandant's patience gave way and our captain received the order to send another patrol. He picked me and I chose King, Delpeuch, and Birchler. All three had automatics, King a *parabellum*, Delpeuch and Birchler, Brownings. They left their rifles, bayonets, and cartridge-boxes behind and in Indian file followed me at a full run in an oblique direction past the front of the company and, when halfway across the clearing, following my example, fell flat on the ground. We rested awhile to regain our wind and then began to slide on our stomachs at right angles to our first course.

We were extremely careful to remain silent. Every little branch and twig we moved carefully out of our way; with one hand extended we felt of the ground before us as we hitched ourselves along. So silent was our progress that several times I felt in doubt about any one being behind me and rested motionless until I felt the touch of Delpeuch's hand upon my foot. After what seemed twenty minutes, we again changed direction, this time straight toward the trees looming close to us. We arrived abreast of the first row of trees, and, lying still as death, listened for sounds of the enemy. All was absolutely quiet; only the branches rustled overhead in a light breeze. A long time we lay there but heard no sound. We began to feel somewhat creepy, and I was tempted to pull my pistol and let nine shots rip into the damnable stillness before us. However, I refrained, and, touching my neighbor, started crawling along the edge of the wood. Extreme care was necessary, owing to the numberless branches littering the ground. The sweat was rolling down my face.

Again we listened, and again we were baffled by that silence. I was angry then and started to crawl between the trees. A tiny sound of metal scratching upon metal and I almost sank into the ground! Quickly I felt reassured. It was my helmet touching a strand of barbed wire. Still no sound!

Boldly we rose and, standing behind trees, scanned the darkness. Over to our right we saw a glimmer of light, and, walking this time, putting one foot carefully before the other, we moved in that direction. When opposite we halted and—I swore. From the supposed trench of the enemy came the hoarse sound of an apparently drunken man singing the *chanson* "La Riviera." Another voice offered a toast to "La Légion."

Carelessly we made our way through the barbed wire, crawling under and stepping over the strands, jumped over a ditch and looked down into what seemed to be an underground palace. There they were—the six men of the One Hundred and Seventy-second—three of them lying stiff and stark on benches, utterly drunk. Two were standing up disputing, and the singer sat in an armchair, holding a long-stemmed glass in his hand. Close by him were several unopened bottles of champagne upon the table. Many empty bottles littered the floor. The singer welcomed us with a shout and an open hand, to which we, however, did not immediately respond. The heartbreaking work while approaching this place rankled in our mind. The sergeant and corporal were too drunk to be of any help, while two of the men were crying, locked in each others' arms. Another was asleep, and our friend the singer absolutely refused to budge. So, after I had stowed two bottles inside my shirt (an example punctiliously followed by the others), we returned.

Leaving Birchler at the wire, I placed King in the middle of the clearing and Delpeuch near the edge of the wood held by us, and then reported. The captain passed the word along to the major, and on the instant we were ordered to fall in, and in column of two marched over to the abandoned trench, following the line marked by my men.

As we entered and disposed ourselves therein, I noticed all the officers, one after the other, disappear in the palace. Another patrol was sent out by our company, and, after ranging the country in our front, it returned safely. That night it happened to be the second company's turn to mount outposts, and we could see six groups of men, one corporal and five men in each, march out into the night, and somewhere, each in some favorable spot, they placed themselves at a distance of about one hundred metres away, to watch, while we slept the sleep of the just.

VIII

Day came, and with it the *corvée* carrying hot coffee and bread. After breakfast another *corvée* was sent after picks and shovels, and the men were set to work remodeling the trench, shifting the parapet to the other side, building little outpost trenches and setting barbed wire. The latter job was done in a wonderfully short time, thanks to German thoroughness, since for the stakes to which the wire is tied the Boches had substituted soft iron rods, three quarters of an inch thick, twisted five times in the shape of a great corkscrew. This screw twisted into the ground exactly like a cork-puller into a cork. The straight part of the rod, being twisted upon itself down and up again every ten inches, formed six or seven small round loops in a height of about five feet. Into these eyes the barbed wire was laid and solidly secured with short lengths of tying wire. First cutting the tying wire, we lifted the barbed wire out of the eyes, shoved a small stick through one and, turning the rod with the leverage of the stick, unscrewed it out of the ground and then reversing the process screwed it in again. The advantage of this rod is obvious. When a shell falls amidst this wire protection, the rods are bent and twisted, but unless broken off short they always support the wire, and even after a severe bombardment present a serious obstacle to the assaulters. In such cases wooden posts are blown to smithereens by the shells, and when broken off let the wire fall flat to the ground.

As I was walking up and down, watching the work, I noticed a large box, resting bottom up, in a deep hole opening from the trench. Dragging the box out and turning it over, I experienced a sudden flutter of the heart. There, before my astonished eyes, resting upon a little platform of boards, stood a neat little centrifugal pump painted green and on the base of it in raised iron letters I read the words "Byron Jackson, San Francisco." I felt queer at the stomach for an instant. San Francisco! my home town! Before my eyes passed pictures of Market Street and the "Park." In fancy I was one of the Sunday crowd at the Cliff House. How could this pump have got so far from home? Many times I had passed the very place where it was made. How, I wonder, did the Boche get this pump? Before the war or through Holland? A California-built pump to clean water out of German trenches, in France! It was astonishing! With something like reverence I put the pump back again and, going to my place in the trench, dug out one of my bottles of champagne and stood treat to the crowd. Somehow, I felt almost happy.

As I continued my rounds I came upon a man sitting on the edge of the ditch surrounded by naked branches, busy cutting them into two-foot lengths and tying them together in the shape of a "cross." I asked him how many he was making, and he told me that he expected to work all day to supply the crosses needed along one battalion front. French and German were treated alike, he assured me. There was absolutely no difference in the size of the crosses.

As we worked, soup arrived, and when that was disposed of, the men rested for some hours. We were absolutely unmolested except by our officers.

But at one o'clock that night we were again assembled in marching rig, each man carrying an extra pick or shovel, and we marched along parallel with our trench to the summit of the butte. There we installed ourselves in the main line out of which the Germans were driven by the One Hundred and Seventy-second. Things came easy now. There was no work of any kind to be done, and quickly we found some dry wood, built small fires and with the material found in dugouts brewed some really delightful beverages. Mine was a mixture of wine and water out of Haeffle's canteen, judiciously blended with chocolate.

The weather was delightful and we spent the afternoon lying in sunny spots, shifting once in a while out of the encroaching shade into the warm rays. We had no idea where the Germans were,—somewhere in front, of course, but just how far or how near mattered little to us. Anyway, the One Hundred and Seventy-second were fully forty metres nearer to them than we were, and we could see and hear the first-line troops picking and shoveling their way into the ground.

Little King was, as usual, making the round of the company, trying to find some one to build a fire and get water if he, King, would furnish the chocolate. He found no takers and soon he laid himself down, muttering about the laziness of the outfit.

Just as we were dozing deliciously, an agonized yell brought every soldier to his feet. Rushing toward the cry, I found a man sitting on the ground, holding his leg below the knee with both hands and moaning as he rocked back and forth. "Je suis blessé! Je suis blessé!" Brushing his hands aside I examined his limb. There was no blood. I took off the leg-band, rolled up his trousers, and discovered no sign of a wound. I asked the man again where the wound was, and he passed his hand over a small red spot on his shin. Just then another man picked up a small piece of shell, and then the explanation dawned upon me. The Germans were shooting at our planes straight above us; a bit of shell had come down and hit our sleeper on the shin-bone. Amid a gale of laughter he limped away to a more sympathetic audience. Several more pieces of iron fell near us. Some fragments were no joking matter, being the entire rear end of three-inch shells weighing, I should think, fully seven pounds.

At 4 P.M. the soup *corvée* arrived. Besides the usual soup we had roast mutton, one small slice per man, and a mixture of white beans, rice, and string beans. There was coffee, and one cup of wine per man, and, best of all, tobacco. As we munched our food our attention was attracted to the sky above by an intense cannonade directed against several of our aeroplanes sailing east. As we looked, more and more of our war-birds appeared. Whipping out my glasses, I counted fifty-two machines. Another man counted sixty. Haeffle had it a hundred. The official report next day stated fifty-nine. They were flying very high and in very open formation, winging due east. The shells were breaking ahead of them and between them. The heaven was studded with hundreds upon hundreds of beautiful little round grayish clouds, each one the nimbus of a bursting shell. With my prismatics glued to my eyes I watched closely for one falling bird. Though it seemed incredible at the moment, not one faltered or turned back. Due east they steered, into the red painted sky. For several minutes after they had sailed out of my sight I could still hear the roar of the guns. Only one machine, the official report said, was shot down, and that one fell on the return trip.

Just before night fell, we all set to work cutting pine branches, and with the tips prepared soft beds for ourselves. Sentries were placed, one man per section, and we laid ourselves down to sleep. The night passed quietly; again the day started with the usual hot coffee and bread. Soup and stew at 10 A.M., and the same again at 4 P.M. One more quiet night and again the following day. We were becoming somewhat restless with the monotony but were cheered by the captain. That night, he told us, we should return to Suippes and there we should re-form the regiment and rest. The programme sounded good, but I felt very doubtful, so many times we had heard the same tale and so many times we had been disappointed. Each day the *corvées* had brought the same news from the kitchen. At least twenty times different telephonists and *agents de liaison* had brought the familiar story. The soup *corvées* assured us that the drivers of the rolling kitchens had orders to hitch up and pull out toward Souain and Suippes. The telephonists had listened to the order transmitted over the wires. The *agents de liaison* had overheard the commandant telling other officers that he had received marching orders and, "*Ma foi!* each time each one was wrong!" So after all, I was not much disappointed when the order came to unmake the sacks.

We stayed that night and all that day, and when the order to march the following evening came, all of us were surprised, including the captain. I was with the One Hundred and Seventy-second at the time, having some fun with a little Belgian. I had come upon him in the dark and had watched him in growing wonder at his actions. There the little fellow was, stamping up and down, every so often stopping, shaking clenched fists in the air, and spouting curses. I asked him what was the matter. "Rien, mon sergent," he replied. "Je m'excite." "Pourquoi?" I demanded. "Ah," he told me, "look,"—pointing out toward the German line,—"out there lies my friend, dead, with three pounds of my chocolate in his *musette*, and when I'm good and mad, I'm going out to get it!" I hope he got it!

That night at seven o'clock we left the hill, marched through Souain four miles to Suippes and sixteen miles farther on, at Saint-Hilaire, we camped. A total of twenty-six miles.

At Suippes the regiment passed in parade march before some officer of the État-Major, and we were counted:—eight hundred and fifty-two in the entire regiment, out of thirty-two hundred who entered the attack on the 25th of September.

THE END